SOUTH COUN

BEHAVIOR SOLUTIONS
for the
HOME *and* COMMUNITY:
*A Handy Reference Guide for
Parents and Caregivers*

BETH AUNE, OTR/L

Behavior Solutions for the Home and Community:
A Handy Reference Guide for Parents and Caregivers

All marketing and publishing rights guaranteed to
and reserved by:

FUTURE HORIZONS INC.

721 W. Abram Street
Arlington, Texas 76013
800-489-0727
817-277-0727
817-277-2270 (fax)
info@FHautism.com
www.FHautism.com

ISBN: 978-1-935274-85-8
Printed in Canada

Dedication

For Wayne Gilpin

Acknowledgments

Thank you, Beth Burt, who conceptualized the first *Behavior Solutions* book. You were the first parent who taught me the value of partnership with parents.

Thank you to my editor, Jennifer Gilpin Yacio, for your patience, faith, and guidance.

Finally, I am full of gratitude, admiration, and love for the numerous parents with whom I am honored to work to help their children. I am continually amazed, motivated, and touched by your diligence, insight, and dedication to search for understanding. Thank you for sharing your uniquely and wonderfully made children with me. I am blessed daily by the evidence of your immeasurable love for them.

Table of Contents

Introduction

As a pediatric occupational therapist, it is an honor and a privilege to work closely with parents and caregivers of children with a variety of special needs. This partnership is a valuable and critical component in helping children develop vital skills for them to be effective and active participants in the daily activities of their lives. Challenges experienced by children with autism spectrum disorder, Sensory Processing Disorder, attention-deficit disorder, attention-deficit/hyperactivity disorder, and other diagnoses must be addressed within the context of the family. This approach is both necessary and beneficial to foster the children's increased independence, improved behavior, and healthy self-image, as well as to promote improved peace and harmony for the entire family at home and in the community.

In my work with children and their families, questions and concerns that consistently require guidance, strategies, and support arise in the areas of:

- Self-care

- Eating and mealtime issues

- Bedtime and sleeping concerns

- Community outings

- Relationships with family and friends

My two previous books, coauthored with Beth Burt and Peter Gennero, *Behavior Solutions for the Inclusive Classroom* and *More Behavior Solutions: In and Beyond the Inclusive Classroom,* focused on providing solutions and strategies for teachers and school personnel. The straightforward format of the books, "What is the behavior, why is it occurring, and what can we do to help?" has been extremely well received and found to be effective by offering practical solutions for challenging behaviors.

Parents, as well as educational professionals, have also expressed a desire to understand why their children exhibit behaviors like meltdowns and overstimulation, rigidity, controlling behaviors, avoidance, disorganization, limited independence during self-care, and decreased social interaction. They are interested in learning and implementing strategies that are practical and relevant to their child's specific needs, with the added element of considering that child within the context of the family's daily life. Comments such as, "I need ideas that don't add more work for me" and "I have three other children—I don't have time to implement a complicated plan" are becoming a theme in my work with parents.

This book, the third in the *Behavior Solutions* series, was conceived in response to those desires. There are numerous, extremely helpful resources for families that delve more deeply into the areas discussed in this book, and some are included in the appendices. This book is intended to provide general, practical solutions for busy (and often overwhelmed) parents who can benefit from a handy reference guide to help them address common behaviors at home and in the community. These solutions have been implemented successfully for years by a multitude of parents and caregivers with whom I have been honored to work, as a partner, to foster their child's growth and progress. This book is a labor of love, dedicated to the families and to the wonderfully unique children who have challenged and inspired me to become a better occupational therapist—and, even more important—a better person.

Part 1

Self-Care and Promoting Independence

It can be very challenging for parents to address a variety of concerns related to their child's abilities or behaviors during dressing tasks. Some children with Sensory Processing Disorder (SPD) have difficulty with motor planning and sequencing: They may have challenges coming up with a plan and don't even initiate the dressing task, or they may exhibit over-reliance on a parent's help. Others may have a plan, but they can't figure out the order of the steps (which is termed *poor sequencing*). Some children want to dress themselves, and they know the correct order of steps, but they lack the necessary motor skills, such as balance, strength, and fine-motor function, to dress themselves effectively in a timely manner. Other children can manage putting on the basic upper-body and lower-body clothing, but they put the items on backward, inside out, or twisted, because they lack awareness of their body senses. These children are described as *sensory under-responsive.* Many children master basic dressing skills but cannot manage small fasteners, such as buttons, snaps, zippers, and tying shoelaces. Some prefer to be underdressed or naked, while others prefer wearing layers or tight clothing. Many children with SPD are very picky about clothing and can be sensitive to certain fabrics, tags, seams, or odors that are present in clothes. These children are described as *sensory over-responsive.* They may avoid and resist dressing and might even have a tantrum at the idea of getting dressed. Many children with autism spectrum disorder may insist on following a theme with their clothing, such as wearing only the color blue or wearing garments with a favorite video or television character on them. Other children are described as *sensory seeking,* and they have a high level of energy and prefer playing, running, and jumping around to slowing down and getting dressed.

Learning how to dress oneself is an important developmental skill that, unfortunately, can be frustrating for both the child and the caregivers. Some parents end up simply dressing their child because it is easier, which can create learned helplessness and over-reliance on assistance. Or, a battle of wills between parent and child can ensue, which can start the day off in a negative way. Fortunately, when parents understand why dressing is challenging, they can develop strategies to encourage the child's increased active participation, willingness, and sense of mastery.

Chapter 1

Getting Dressed

Many children can be described as *sensory under-responsive*. They lack awareness of general body senses and appear clumsy and uncoordinated. They can seem aimless, disorganized, and distracted. The children may try to dress themselves, but parents end up completing the task because it takes too long. Some children have attention-deficit/hyperactivity disorder (ADHD) or are *sensory seeking*. They prefer to run and jump around and have difficulty calming down to get dressed. Conflict can arise, and the day starts off poorly because the family is rushing around and there is a sense of chaos.

Solutions

● Allow more time for dressing in the mornings, to encourage increased participation and discourage over-reliance on assistance from the adult.

● Establish a consistent routine that is easy to follow.

● Use a visual checklist, with pictures, to support the routine. Encourage your child to refer to it, to decrease her need for verbal reminders and increase her level of independence.

- Have your child choose her clothes and lay them out the night before.

- Get dressed in an area without enticing distractions, such as toys, television, and computers.

- Have your sensory under-responsive child engage in a "wake up your body" activity (see Appendix A) to raise awareness of the body senses prior to dressing and improve motor skills.

- A "calm your body" activity (see Appendix A) can be used prior to dressing tasks to help your child be more attentive.

- When working with your child to be more independent, try working with her at night or on the weekends, when there is not a time restriction to get out of the house.

- Use the backward chaining approach (see Appendix B) to help your child develop motor skills, decrease dependence on the caregiver, and decrease frustration levels.

- Obtain services from a pediatric occupational therapist if your child exhibits significant delays with development of self-care skills.

Chapter 2

Restricted Clothing Choices

Some children are very sensitive to certain types of sensation. These children can be categorized as *sensory over-responsive,* because they overreact to sensory input and can become emotional. In the area of dressing, both the tactile (touch) and the olfactory (smell) sensory input can be interpreted as uncomfortable, irritable, and even painful. They are overly aware of and sensitive to touch and odors. The "new clothes" smell that others don't notice is often overwhelming to these children. The feeling and pressure of tags, seams, waistbands, shoelaces, and textures are irritants to their skin. The behaviors these children exhibit include crying, refusing to get dressed or wear certain items, throwing a tantrum, preferring to be underdressed, or demonstrating rigidity. In addition to sensory sensitivities, some children become rigid about their clothing choices. For most, this is an attempt to regain power and control over their world and to restore a sense of order and consistency, because their responses to various stimuli from the environment and their own bodies are disorganized, uncomfortable, and unpredictable. It is important to recognize sensory sensitivities and be aware that these children are very uncomfortable with their bodies and their brain's interpretations and responses to sensory input. As a result, they can exhibit challenging behaviors that require compassion, patience, and consistency.

Solutions

- Wash new clothes several times before wearing them.

- Cut out tags and try to buy clothes that have few, flat, or no seams.

- Have your child choose his own clothing. Take note of the type of fabric, fit, and style he prefers.

- Pick your battles. Does it really matter if your child will only wear blue?

- Think "outside the box" and try something untraditional, such as letting your child sleep in his school clothes. Many children are less sensitive in the evening after a bath, as compared to first thing in the morning.

- Give your child a reward and positive reinforcement for trying to wear different clothing, even for short periods of time.

- Try letting your child wear a comfortable, well-accepted shirt under a new shirt.

● Turning underwear or socks inside out keeps the un-comfortable sensation of the seams away from the skin.

Chapter 3

Buttoning, Snapping, and Zipping

Managing fasteners and closures for clothing requires dexterity and coordination of the small muscles of the hands, use of the two hands together, established hand dominance, good motor planning, and a high frustration tolerance. Children with disabilities struggle in many, if not all, of these areas. They may have poor muscle tone, poor joint stability, reduced sensory registration of finger position, and poor manipulative skills. It is important to remember that fine-motor functions are the last motor skills to develop and to keep in mind that these skills require developmental readiness, as well as motivation to persist. Some children can learn to button, snap, and zip with assistance and practice, but others may need accommodations or modifications.

Solutions

- For front-closure items, such as shirts with buttons or jackets with zippers, snaps, or buttons, have your child place the item on the floor or the bed face up and fasten it three-quarters of the way up, then put it on his body in the same manner as a pullover shirt or sweatshirt.

● Place a pull tag or ring on zippers to allow him to pull the zipper up more easily.

● Practice buttoning, zipping, and snapping with the clothes off the body, rather than on. This enlists the aid of the visual system and reduces frustration levels.

● When practicing with clothes off the body, be sure to orient the garment on the floor or table in the same direction as your child's body to avoid right/left hand confusion.

● Master larger buttons before moving on to smaller ones.

● Replace buttons or slide-closures on slacks or shorts with Velcro. Then sew the button onto the outside flap.

Chapter 4

Tying Shoelaces

When adults find themselves in the situation of trying to teach a child a dressing task, it is often surprising how difficult it can be. Tying shoelaces, as with other daily activities, is a habitual act that adults have been doing for so long, it isn't something that requires conscious thought. We can truly "do it with our eyes closed." The act of tying shoelaces is stored in our motor memory, so breaking it down into steps to teach it can be quite difficult. Then, take into consideration that our children don't have the necessary skills of being able to pay attention, sequence steps, coordinate both hands to work together, execute fine-motor dexterity, and demonstrate visual perceptual function. No wonder it is so frustrating for both the parent and the child! As in the former chapter, many children are able to learn to tie their shoelaces, but some may need accommodations.

Solutions

- Try using the "bunny ears" technique, with a modification in the first step.

» Hold the shoelaces 1"-2" from the shoe, not at the ends.

» Cross the right lace behind the left one if the child is right handed. Cross the left lace behind right one if he is left handed. This will make an "X."

» It can be helpful to mark the laces with dots to help the child line them up together.

» Use the other, nondominant hand to pinch and hold the laces where they cross at the "X."

» Instruct the child that this is the "stay put" (non-dominant) hand, which won't move. This keeps him from dropping the laces and crossing his hands.

» Next, the "working hand" (dominant hand) tucks the lace on the same side as the dominant hand, through the space from behind, at the bottom of the "X," pulling it in the direction of the dominant hand (the arm will be moving away from, not crossing, the body).

» *Do this step twice.* This will keep the laces tight for the next step.

» Form two short loops ("bunny ears"), and cross them. Pinch them into place with the "stay put" hand, and feed the right loop through from behind and under, pulling it in the direction of the dominant hand.

» When teaching a child how to tie shoelaces, make sure the child has the first step mastered before moving on to the bunny ears.

» Initially, a parent may need to form the laces or loops and cross them, then have the child pinch the "X" and pull the laces or loop through to tighten.

» Give enough assistance to keep your child from becoming overly frustrated, but not so much that he simply lets you do it.

This technique is effective because it keeps the child from dropping the laces and crossing his arms over each other. The bunny ears step involves the exact motor sequence of the first step.

The following are modifications to tying shoelaces:

● Velcro closures are alternatives, if they are age appropriate.

● Slip-on shoes, such as Vans, are options.

● Modified laces, such as Lock Laces, Hickies Elastic Lacing System, and Slack Laces, are helpful and encourage independence.

● Some shoes are slip-on but have a faux laces style.

Chapter 5

Bathing and Showering

The challenges associated with taking a bath or shower can vary from child to child. Some children enjoy this time so much that they refuse to get out of the bathtub or shower, or they spend an excessive amount of time in the bathroom. This can create added stress and conflict in the home and delay bedtime or morning departure. Some children exhibit fearful reactions to having the sensation of water on their faces, tipping their heads back to rinse out shampoo, hearing the sound of water running, having the sensation of soap on their skin, or seeing the water drain out of the bathtub. The fearful reactions are seen most often in children who are overly sensitive to light touch or have vestibular over-responsivity to head movement, which intensifies when the head is tipped backward. The sensory-seeking child may tumble around in the bathtub, splash water out onto the floor, suck on wet washcloths, or even try to eat or taste soap and shampoo.

- Set a timer for bath time to encourage the child to bathe or shower in a timely manner.

- Use a "first/then" approach to help the child who won't get out of the tub or shower or the child who avoids bath time. For example: "First, take your bath, then you can [insert a highly preferred activity]." This aids the child in terminating the bath and transitioning more easily.

- Place a visor on your child's head prior to shampooing and rinsing, to keep water out of his face.

- Encourage your child to tip his head forward to rinse shampoo in the bathtub or shower. This won't stimulate an over-reactive response to head position changes, compared with tipping the head backward.

- For a child who is sensitive to the sound of the water running, fill the bathtub or start the shower when he is away from the bathroom.

- Have the sensory-seeking child or the child with ADHD engage in movement activities prior to bath time to decrease excessive splashing.

- Keep the lights dim, play soft music, and provide scents such as jasmine, lavender, and chamomile to calm the child. This calming strategy is effective for both the sensory seeker and the sensitive, sensory over-responsive child.

• Help your child identify soap and shampoo that feel comfortable on his skin and smell good to him.

• Encourage the highest level of independence possible. Having your child wash his own body and hair will give an overly active child more appropriate movement options, and it will give a sensitive child a feeling of control.

Chapter 6

Haircuts and Grooming

Getting haircuts and grooming hair are especially difficult for children with sensory sensitivities and children with autism spectrum disorder (ASD). The sensation of tiny hairs falling onto the neck and face, the sound of scissors or clippers cutting the hair, and the bright fluorescent lights in hair salons can be overwhelming. Some children with ASD have difficulty adjusting to their "new look." Hair combing or brushing can feel uncomfortable and even painful to some children. The sensation and odor of hair gels are often perceived as noxious. These children can exhibit behaviors such as screaming, crying, clinging to a parent or caregiver, and running away. Some children want to brush or comb their own hair, but their motor skills are not developed enough to do a thorough job, and attempts by the parent to assist the child are met with resistance and arguing.

Solutions

- The overly sensitive and anxious child may require calming activities prior to haircuts and grooming.

Attempts to groom and give haircuts when a child is overly agitated are rarely successful.

● Try cutting your child's hair in the bathtub. Children are often in a calm state in the tub and are less likely to be anxious during the haircut.

● Wet the hair, either in the bathtub or out of it. Wet hair will come off in chunks and won't tickle and irritate the neck as it falls.

● If fluorescent lights are an issue during the haircut, allow your child to wear sunglasses.

● Allow the child to wear ear buds during the haircut. Play her favorite music to help her tune out the sound of scissors or clippers.

● Avoid the use of clippers with the child who is sensitive to the sound and vibration. Use scissors, instead.

● Try counting or singing while combing and brushing your child's hair to give her a clear sense of the beginning and end of the task.

● Try taking turns and letting her brush or comb your hair. Then you brush hers to encourage her to accept your assistance.

● Provide a positive reinforcement or reward after a successful grooming session. Validate your child's participation.

Chapter 7

Brushing Teeth

Many parents and caregivers report that the seemingly simple act of brushing the teeth ends up in a huge battle. This is a daily living skill that is vital for good oral hygiene and preserving the teeth. Many children react to the sight of the toothbrush by running away, crying, refusing to open their mouths, and covering their mouths. Often, parents must resort to holding their child and "just getting it over with." The tickling sensation of the toothbrush and the taste, odor, and feel of the toothpaste can be perceived as uncomfortable and even painful to some children. Others will allow the toothbrush inside the mouth, but they will simply eat the toothpaste and chew on the toothbrush bristles. Some kids don't experience sensory sensitivities, but their hand skills are not yet coordinated enough to brush their teeth with efficiency and thoroughness.

Solutions

- Desensitize the mouth area prior to making attempts at brushing teeth. Use a playful method. Blow raspberries and gently fill the child's cheeks with air.

Push it out with your fingers to make silly sounds. Let your child touch your face first, and then you can touch his.

● Experiment with different types of toothbrushes. Some children enjoy or prefer the sensation of electric brushes, while others need a manual toothbrush.

● Use unflavored, odorless toothpaste.

● Some children may tolerate tooth brushing with water only. Start with this, and, when tolerance increases, slowly add very small amounts of toothpaste.

● Invent a brushing-teeth song to sing during brushing. This will distract your child, while providing him with a clear understanding of the beginning and end of the task.

● Use a predictable sequence when you brush: top right, top front, top left, bottom left, bottom middle, bottom right. Keep the toothbrush in the mouth and in contact with the teeth, avoiding a "start and stop" pattern.

● When assisting a child who has poor motor skills, hold the end of the toothbrush or your child's forearm to help guide it, rather than placing your hand over your child's. This will encourage him to more actively develop his hand functioning.

Chapter 8

Cutting Fingernails and Toenails

There are several reasons why children have negative behavioral responses to clipping or cutting fingernails and toenails. For some, it is the sound of the clipping utensil that is irritating. For others, the pressure and touch sensation on the tips of the toes and fingers is uncomfortable. As with any imposed touch by a caregiver, it is very challenging for kids to anticipate how long they must endure it, how it will feel, and what to expect. Once a child has a negative experience during an event such as cutting nails, he often reacts by simply refusing to allow his parent or caregiver to trim them. Similar to brushing teeth, some parents are put into the unhappy situation of "forcing" their child to have his nails trimmed, which creates anxiety and unhappiness for everyone involved.

Solutions

- For the child with auditory sensitivity, try trimming the nails with nail scissors, rather than clippers, to eliminate the "clipping" sound.

- Try trimming nails when your child is calm, such as in the bathtub or even while he's sleeping.

- Trimming nails after the hands or feet are wet reduces the sound of the clipping.

- Count from 1 to 10 while trimming the nails, by using a closed-ended and predictable routine.

- Some children will allow the use of an emery board to shorten or file the nails.

- Teach your child how to use the scissors or clippers by letting him cut your nails or a willing sibling's nails first. Then, when he has mastered the motor component, he can cut his own.

- Cut the nails while your child is happily distracted by a favorite video or song or while he is eating.

Chapter 9

Lotions and Sunscreens

Many parents are aware of "tactile sensitivity," which means a child is overly sensitive to certain types of touch. Light touch is often perceived as ticklish and is overly alerting, while deep-pressure touch is more comfortable. Until a lotion is rubbed in, it may feel slimy and irritating. The reaction to the sensation of lotions on the skin can be extreme, eliciting hitting, kicking, screaming, crying, running away, and high levels of anxiety. In addition to the more commonly understood concept of tactile defensiveness, many children are very sensitive to odors. Reactions based on the sense of smell are almost always emotional ones and shouldn't be overlooked. In addition to an over-reaction to the feel and smell of lotions and sunscreens, some children are sensitive to the temperature change involved when applying these products. The temperature difference between a cool lotion and warm skin can stimulate a negative behavioral response.

- When possible, allow your child to put lotion on his own body. Only he knows what type of touch feels best and how long he can endure the touch.

- Some children don't like the feel of lotions on their own hands, but they will tolerate it on their bodies. They can wear gloves or put the lotion on a nonabsorbent cloth to rub it in.

- Don't put cold lotion on a warm body right after bath time. Try warming the lotion to the same temperature as the body first.

- Start by applying lotions to the least sensitive areas of the body, such as the legs or back.

- Use very firm, consistent, and deep pressure during lotion application, and keep your hand in contact with your child's skin.

- Provide a soothing, calm verbal dialogue during application: "Right leg, left leg, stomach, right arm, left arm, back," so your child knows what to expect. Keep the pattern predictable from one day to the next.

- Use swim shirts to keep your child's body covered during swimming.

● Work with your child to find out which lotions smell the best to him and which textures are acceptable. Some lotions have a greasy feeling and don't soak into the skin as well as others.

Chapter 10

Using the Toilet

Using the toilet can involve many different issues, including toilet training, sensory concerns, motor skills, and motivation. There are many helpful resources (see Additional Resources on page 143) to address toilet training. This chapter will offer solutions and strategies to help foster readiness for using the toilet and to address sensory issues your toilet-trained child may have. One area that can be overlooked is postural control. Some children become fearful and agitated when their feet are off the ground while they are seated on the toilet. They can be insecure if they are standing on a step stool or feel as if they may fall into the toilet because the seat is too large. Others are fearful of the sound of the toilet flushing, which is sometimes very loud in public places. In addition, many public restrooms have a concrete floor and high ceilings, so sounds are magnified. Ceiling fans can be an auditory irritant or a visual distraction. Some children don't like the sensation of water splashing on their bare bottoms after having bowel movements. On the other hand, many children perseverate on toilet flushing, use too much toilet paper, and throw items into the toilet.

- Make sure your child is comfortable and secure while sitting on the toilet by giving him a footstool to rest his feet on or something to hold on to, such as a bar on the wall.

- Bring a favorite book or toy into the restroom to distract him and keep him happy while sitting on the toilet.

- Consider letting him sit backward, facing the back of the toilet, to help him feel more secure with his posture and to have something to hold on to with his arms.

- Teach him to cover his ears and give him forewarning with the sound of the toilet flushing, or let him leave the bathroom while you flush.

- Work on desensitizing his reaction to the toilet flushing. Start by letting your child flush, then count to "one," then flush and count to "two," then "three," and so on.

- Disable loud ceiling fans if they stimulate your child's anxiety.

- Put a padded ring on the toilet seat for small children, to narrow the opening of the toilet.

● If splashing after having a bowel movement is an issue, lower the level of the water in the bowl.

● Use flushable wipes to enhance toilet hygiene. These will provide thorough cleanliness and keep the child from using too much toilet paper.

Part II

Eating and Mealtime at Home

Many cultures associate eating with nurturing and socializing with others. When problems with mealtime arise at home, parents can feel discouraged and disappointed. Behaviors associated with eating and mealtimes can be very challenging for parents, who often find themselves feeling anxious, frustrated, and overwhelmed during mealtimes or even when anticipating the meal. Negative patterns that can develop between child and caregiver can include avoidance, arguing, pleading, bribing, and excessive time and attention spent with the child during meals. These commonly reported concerns could disrupt the entire family, create chaos, and leave parents feeling unsuccessful.

Some children have severely restricted food choices due to texture intolerance, and they exhibit behaviors such as refusing to try new foods, spitting food out, gagging, and even vomiting. They may be nutritionally deprived or underweight. Parents of these children can feel pressured to help their child gain weight, and they dread going to annual checkups at the pediatrician's office. Other children may eat large amounts of food, but their repertoire is limited to simple, soft carbohydrates that are easy to chew because they don't have the oral muscle strength required for chewing meats or other solid foods. Some children are messy eaters who have poor fine-motor skills for utensil use or drinking from an open cup; they may start a meal by using a spoon or fork, and then begin to eat with their hands because it is more efficient. An orally under-aware child will overstuff his mouth and have a poor bite-chew-swallow pacing pattern. A sensory-seeking child may play with or throw his food, refuse to sit in a chair to eat, or sit for a brief period before running away from the table.

This section offers some immediate and practical solutions and strategies to address common behaviors. The "Additional Resources" section on page 143 provides more extensive information to help with severe feeding concerns.

Chapter 11

Trouble with Textures

Some children have great difficulty transitioning from pureed or soft foods to foods with mixed textures or solid foods. These children are more sensitive to the feeling of foods on their lips and in their mouths. They may have a hypersensitive gag reflex, which can be triggered as soon as food enters the mouth and touches the tongue or when they attempt to swallow. Premature infants commonly experience challenges with eating textured foods when they are introduced, as do children who exhibit sensory over-responsiveness to touch and other sensations. These children can have difficulty gaining weight and thriving. On the other hand, some children may prefer or insist upon eating only solid foods that are crunchy, spicy, or chewy, and they will gag on foods that feel too soft or "slimy" in their mouths. Some will eat only cold foods, while others prefer room-temperature foods or very hot ones.

- If your child is overly sensitive and anxious about eating, it is important to help him achieve a calm state prior to feeding.

- When introducing new foods, take an inventory of the foods that your child will eat and identify what is common to those foods (flavor, texture, color, smell). Give him a new food that shares those attributes to increase his willingness to try the new food.

- Introduce only one new option at a time, so he won't become overwhelmed and shut down.

- Before the sensitive child eats, try desensitizing the mouth and lip area by using a playful method. You can blow raspberries and gently fill her cheeks with air. Then push it out with your fingers to make silly sounds.

- Allow her to eat with distractions, such as watching a favorite video. This will reduce her anxiety level and help her to not obsess or hyperfocus on eating.

- Avoid giving too much attention (both negative and positive) to eating or inadvertently "pressuring" your child to eat.

● Try taking turns eating bites of food with your child, or enlist the help of a willing sibling or friend to make mealtimes more fun and social.

● Have reasonable expectations for the amount of food you would like your child to eat, and make sure she clearly understands the expectation.

● Don't put too much food on one plate—this can create an immediate shutdown response. Try using smaller plates or bowls with just a few bites, and then fill the plate or bowl again to make the task of eating more manageable.

Chapter 12

Restricted Diet and Picky Eating

While it is developmentally expected that children may have a limited food repertoire during the toddler years, some may continue to insist upon eating a limited choice of foods, which is concerning to parents and caregivers. Adults can overlook the fact that they, too, may have a "menu" of food options they prefer and gravitate toward. It is important to differentiate between a limited diet that lacks necessary nutritional value and a diet that has a limited repertoire but is nutritionally sound.

Often, mealtimes turn into battlegrounds, with parent and child locked into a battle of wills to gain power and control. For children that experience a day full of sensory overload, disorganization, and dysregulation, becoming rigid about what and when he eats helps him regain a sense of control and calm.

Solutions

- Make a food inventory for the week and analyze your child's intake. You may find that, although his choices are limited, the major food groups are represented.

- When encouraging acceptance of and trying new foods, introduce just one new food at a time, one bite at a time. Repeat that same new food for 10 meals before introducing the next new food.

- Start by telling your child that he doesn't need to eat the food. Let him get used to it by seeing, smelling, and touching it without the pressure of eating it.

- Introduce new foods that are similar in texture, taste, and appearance to the ones your child is currently eating to optimize acceptance and willingness to try them.

- Try not to hover near your child when he is eating.

- Play a game such as "Ring for Mommy or Daddy." Give your child three small bites on a plate, supply him with a bell or ringer, and tell him to "ring the bell" when he's finished. Give him praise for eating!

- Have your child help prepare his meals and snacks. This will give him additional time to explore the food, as well as a sense of independence in choosing his own foods.

Chapter 13

Messy Eating

Meals and snacks can be a virtual smorgasbord of opportunity for a sensory-seeking child to smash, squeeze, spit, swish, and throw food. Some kids rub food onto clothing, hands, face, and hair. Others pull it apart, inspect every bite, and smell it. While this is typical behavior for a child who is beginning to finger feed, it is not very charming in older children. They may eventually eat all their food, but their bodies, the table, the chairs, and the floor look as if a bomb exploded. Drinking liquids can also be problematic for sensory-seeking kids, who will blow bubbles with straws, take a drink, and spray it out in the direction of a sibling. Or, they will mix liquids with solid food bites and play with it in their mouths.

The sensory under-responsive child can also be messy, but for a reason other than exploring the variety of sensory options that food and drinks provide. This child simply lacks tactile awareness of food on his clothing, hands, and face. Visually, he may not differentiate the plate from the table surface. He may lack an awareness of the force behind his movements and have trouble grading liquid flow while drinking from an open cup, resulting in spillage. This child often knocks silverware off the table or tips cups over because he is clumsy and underaware of the space between the table surface and the edge of the table.

Solutions

- Limit the amount of food that is on one plate and give your child small portions to eat. Then, you can give him more when he is finished.

- Offer foods that are less likely to have layers or that can be pulled apart.

- Praise and reward your child for not playing with his food—catch him in "good behavior."

- Identify when he has eaten a sufficient amount, and have him take his plate to the sink before he starts exploring the food and playing with it.

- Take the cup of liquid away from him, in between sips.

- Use a brightly colored placemat to help him see more easily where his plate of food and cup are located.

- Use bowls and plates with suction cups on the bottoms to keep them firmly placed on the tabletop.

- Teach and encourage the use of napkins or moist towelettes. Have him wipe face and hands in between each bite to help slow the pace of feeding and raise awareness of having a clean face and hands.

- Provide heavier feeding utensils and cups to increase sensory feedback and reduce the use of excessive force behind feeding movements.

Chapter 14

Overstuffing the Mouth

A child who has decreased awareness of his mouth is one who will often take two to four large bites of food before his brain registers the sensation of having the food in his mouth. By the time he notices the food, the amount in his mouth becomes difficult to chew and swallow with ease. He might chew and chomp with an open mouth, take some food out with his fingers, or use his fingers to move the food back toward his throat to swallow. He may even spit the food out onto the plate or table.

Solutions

- Cut finger foods such as sandwiches, pizza, and burritos into bites.

- Have the child use a fork or spoon, rather than his hands, to eat. This will help with pacing and decrease overstuffing.

- Start with putting just two bites on a plate at a time, and then increase the number of bites as his pacing improves.

● Encourage the use of a napkin or wet wipe between bites to keep him from taking too many bites before chewing and to aid rhythm. Verbally cue him: "Bite, chew, swallow, wipe your mouth. Bite, chew, swallow, wipe your mouth."

● Give him foods that offer increased sensory stimulation to raise awareness of his mouth. Examples would be beef or turkey jerky, popcorn, ice chips, hot sauce, or lemonade. These types of food and beverage add flavor (spicy, savory, sour, salty) and texture (chewy, crunchy).

● Encourage him to take a drink of milk, water, or juice in between bites to aid in swallowing the food and clearing his mouth.

● Your child may need professional help from an occupational therapist or speech therapist that specializes in oral-motor and oral sensory treatment.

Chapter 15

Utensil Use

The physical act of feeding is something often taken for granted by parents and caregivers. They have been feeding themselves daily for so long that it requires little or no effort or concentration. However, several skills are necessary to learn and master the sequence of holding and using a spoon or fork. This involves holding the utensil in the correct position, scooping or stabbing a bite of food, moving the utensil from the plate or bowl to the mouth, and returning it to the plate for the next bite. In addition to the motor coordination, the child must have intact sensory processing to be able to sense and figure out where to hold the utensil, the force necessary to maintain a grasp, and an understanding of how far the hand holding the utensil is from the plate and the mouth.

The next factor to consider is frustration tolerance. Many children can become easily frustrated when they are trying to master new life skills. They may exhibit negative behaviors, such as throwing utensils, beginning a meal by using a utensil but reverting to using the hands to eat, over-reliance on an adult's assistance, and learned helplessness.

- Avoid using a "hand-over-hand" approach to assist your child. She will merely let you do the work for her, and you won't be able to determine which part of the sequence she can perform independently.

- Instead, watch your child and give your assistance only during the step where she needs it. She may be able to hold the spoon and scoop, but she needs guidance to bring it to her mouth to keep it facing upward.

- Hold the end of the spoon or the fork to assist your child, or guide her at the wrist or forearm to help her achieve success.

- During feeding with a spoon, start with foods that will stick to and stay on the spoon easily, such as mashed potatoes, pudding, or yogurt.

- Increase the likelihood of persistence by teaching utensil use with highly preferred foods.

- Prolonged challenges with utensil use can be addressed by an occupational therapist that is skilled at task analysis and promoting independence in life skills.

Chapter 16

Sitting at the Table and Staying in the Seat

Sensory-seeking children and those with ADHD generally have difficulty sitting still for prolonged periods. They may start a meal by sitting down, but they may shift their seated position frequently, tip the chair back, swing and kick their legs while sitting, or run back and forth between the table and another room. Some children with ASD or sensory over-responsivity might experience sensory sensitivities and react by being anxious or avoidant, and they may run away from the table. The competing odors, sounds of other people chewing, scraping noises of metal utensils on ceramic plates, and simultaneous conversations of family members can create sensory overload. Some may feel postural insecurity if their feet don't touch the ground while they're seated in a large chair.

- Provide movement opportunities prior to mealtime to help your child stay calm while eating (see Appendix A).

- Allow your fidgety child to stand, rather than sit, to eat—as long as he stays at the table.

- Place a resistive exercise band around the legs of his chair to reduce kicking and calm restless legs.

- Be realistic about your expectations for sitting. If your child has completed his meal, allow him to ask to be excused, rather than remain at the table and create chaos for other family members.

- Some children have "met their limit" for socialization by being at school all day or undergoing various therapies. They may need a quiet place to enjoy their meal.

- Your sensitive child may benefit from using headphones or ear buds with music to decrease the auditory input at the table.

- Provide a booster chair or a stool for your child's feet to help him feel safe and supported at the table.

Chapter 17

Swallowing Medication and Supplements

There are several challenges associated with medication, vitamins, and supplements. Some children are extremely sensitive to odors, and no matter how creative parents are in their attempts to hide medication or supplements in food, the children notice and refuse to take it. Learning to swallow pills is hard for children with deficits in oral-motor function or those with oral hypersensitivity. Often, if a child has one negative experience with medication, he will adamantly refuse to try again. He will run away, cover his mouth, clench his teeth and lips together, and become anxious or upset.

Solutions

- Use a small syringe to distribute liquid medication in tiny amounts in a favorite food that has a strong taste and odor, such as peanut butter cookies or a brownie.

- Specialty health food stores carry odorless supplements, such as tuna oil for omega-3 supplements.

● CAUTION: Only children that have no issues with choking and who can swallow liquids safely should practice swallowing pills.

● When teaching a willing child to swallow a pill, it is vital to prompt him to keep his chin down, rather than tipping the head back. This will keep the esophagus open and aid in swallowing.

● Place the pill on the center of your child's tongue and instruct him to drink a cup of water as he usually does.

● Try having your child use a straw to drink the water and wash the pill down. This way, he can focus on drinking from the straw, rather than swallowing the pill.

● Have your child practice swallowing mini-M&M's, Tic Tac mints, or small candy balls found in the cake-decorating section of the grocery store.

● Special cups are available to aid in swallowing pills. An example is the OralFlo Pill Swallowing cup.

Part III

Bedtime and Sleeping

There are several challenging behaviors associated with bedtime and sleeping. Some children, such as sensory seekers and those with ADHD or ASD, seem to have boundless energy throughout the day, and it may even increase as bedtime nears. They struggle with the ability to achieve a quiet, calm state and have challenges with following a bedtime routine and going to bed. Parents are very aware of the necessity to help their children get a solid night's sleep, to allow them to have effective functioning the next day at school and at home. But, parents have significant challenges getting their child into bed. Teachers may report that a student consistently falls asleep at school or is difficult to engage. Children may have behavioral issues due to lack of sleep and feeling out of sorts. Other children may go to bed without difficulty, but they don't sleep throughout the night. Noises such as dogs barking, sprinklers starting, cars driving by, and even the wind blowing can wake them up because their hearing is so sensitive. Many children that don't get enough sleep will struggle with waking up in the morning, which creates stress for parents who are on a timeline and have to help their children get on the bus or in the car to get to school. This sets a negative tone in the family home; the emotional energy level is high, and starting the day off rushed and feeling pressured may increase the child's arousal and result in a disorganized state or anxious mood. Other children, such as those with ASD, may have a rigid, ritualistic bedtime or morning routine that simply takes too much time and is disruptive to other family members.

Chapter 18

Waking Up

Mornings for families can be very stressful and pressured. Parents are faced with the daunting tasks of waking their children up, making breakfast and encouraging their children to eat it, packing lunches, checking that backpacks are ready and packed, getting their children dressed, and getting themselves ready to go—all in a limited period of time. When a child is unusually drowsy in the morning and difficult to wake, the entire family goes into "hurry up" mode, which starts the day off in a negative and unhappy way. For children with special needs, this can set a tone that is difficult to recover from, and they have difficulties throughout their school day. Teachers report that these children have short attention spans, seem distracted, may sleep at school, or are emotionally labile. The extremely active child may not have finally gone to bed until 3 hours past bedtime, so when morning comes, he has not had enough sleep. As a result, he is difficult to rouse and is slow to follow his morning schedule.

- Add extra time in the morning and begin by opening your child's door, turning the lights on, and playing lively music to begin to alert him.

- Give him cold water or another favorite beverage to drink, first thing upon waking.

- If possible, have the child who is difficult to wake take his shower in the morning, rather than the evening.

- Use body wash and shampoo with scents that are alerting, such as citrus and mint.

- Have your child use a mesh "scrubby" to wash his body. This will alert the senses through his tactile system.

- Engage your child in a playful movement activity, such as playing "tag" or jumping on a trampoline to get his body moving.

- Provide breakfast foods that give a lot of input to the mouth, such as crunchy, salty, savory, and spicy foods, to help with alerting in the morning.

- Play lively music during the morning routine.

Chapter 19

Getting Out of the House On Time

Leaving the house on time in the morning is problematic for most parents, even if they don't have a child with special needs. Last-minute duties, such as folding a load of laundry, answering an e-mail, doing the dishes, making beds, and having a telephone conversation or texting, seem to be ever present in our busy world. Getting out of the house on time is even more difficult if a parent has a child that insists on watching the credits to his morning television show or video or one who can never seem to find his clothes or backpack quickly. Suddenly, it is time to go, and some parents resort to cajoling or even yelling at their child, and the day starts off unsatisfactorily.

Solutions

- Limit or eliminate the use of electronics in the morning (for both parents and children).

• Look at the morning duties and identify what can be done the night before to streamline the morning preparations.

• Consider making lunches, laying out clothing, and packing backpacks at night.

• The night before, load the car with items that need to go to school.

• Add more time into the morning routine to account for unexpected events. Getting up even 10-15 minutes earlier may be just enough to help the morning go more smoothly.

• Give your ritualistic child enough time to complete his morning routine. Shutting off a video before it is finished may stimulate a 30-minute meltdown that will delay departure even more.

• Provide a visual checklist (see Appendix C) to help your child stay on task and follow a predictable schedule.

Chapter 20

Calming Down for Bedtime

Children who are sensory seeking, have ADHD, and are overly active have great difficulty making the transition to bedtime. Unfortunately, the activity level of the entire household in the evenings can contribute to the restlessness and hyperactivity. Often, the television is on, telephones are ringing, siblings are asking for help with homework, meal preparation can be noisy, various family members are talking loudly to one another, and parents can be distracted by caring for a young infant who may be fussing and crying. This environment will create a higher level of energy and disorganization for the active child, and it will create anxiety, distress, and sensory overload for the sensitive child. For parents who have had a long and stressful day, it can be very challenging to not escalate right along with their child, and they can unwittingly add to the environmental chaos by rushing around or calling across the room to gain their children's attention.

Solutions

- First, try to keep the home environment as calm and quiet as possible.

- Examine how you can reduce the stimulation—perhaps by leaving the television off, turning telephone ringers down, and lowering the lights.

- Play soft, classical music that is calming.

- Model a quiet voice and calm demeanor. Children who are overly stimulated won't be able to focus on your words, but they will respond to your actions.

- When instructing your child, move close to him and ensure you have his attention prior to talking to him. This will help him "listen the first time" and decrease your frustration level.

- Keep the nighttime routine predictable and as simple as possible.

- Use visual checklists (see Appendix D) to decrease your verbal prompting, which may be adding to the auditory chaos.

- Keep bath time quiet and calm by lowering the lights, lighting scented candles, and playing quiet music.

- Use lavender, jasmine, and chamomile scents for candles, soaps, bath salts, body wash, and lotions. These scents are calming.

- Avoid engaging in nondirected roughhouse play or circular spinning, which contributes to a high arousal state.

- Encourage "heavy-work" games and tasks to help calm your child's body, such as carrying the groceries in, vacuuming, or crawling through tunnels or under chairs. See Appendix A for more options.

- Help your child design a "chill out" or "calm down" area in the house to reduce his stimulation level. This is effective for both active and sensitive children.

- Help your child engage in closed-ended, repetitive tasks that do not have a high level of cognitive effort, such as sorting the laundry or silverware, playing with Legos, assembling puzzles, and engaging in sorting and matching activities.

- Consult with your pediatrician about options to aid sleep, such as taking melatonin or medication, if the problem is significant and persistent.

Chapter 21

Inconsistent Sleep Patterns

Some children may go to bed without any difficulty one night, then refuse to go to bed the next night. Others might go to bed, sleep for a few hours, and then wake up. Some parents report that their child seems to have sleep problems that are cyclical in nature, such as during the full moon. This is in contrast to the sensory-seeking child, for example, who consistently exhibits the same problematic behavior of not calming down to get to bed or to sleep. A sensory over-responsive child may be fearful, hypervigilant, controlling, or anxious, and these behaviors increase with stress from school or home.

As simple as it may sound, it is vital to implement a consistent bedtime routine for children that exhibit inconsistent behaviors. Parents often feel uncertain and can't develop strategies because they never know quite what to expect, and they fall into a reactive pattern of responding on the basis of the child's current behavior.

- Try to think and behave in a proactive, rather than reactive, manner. If your responses to your child are variable, this will just add to his disorganized and inconsistent behaviors.

- When at all possible, keep bedtime the same from night to night.

- Help your child identify a bedtime routine that works for him. Incorporating his participation will make it more meaningful, and he will more easily remember his bedtime sequence if he helped develop it. This will reduce anxiety about the expectations for bedtime.

- Help your child make a poster or chart and use his terminology and words to describe his nighttime routine.

- Keep the bedroom peaceful by using blackout shades, playing soft classical music, or introducing "white noise," such as a fan.

- Position the bed against a wall, rather than in the center of the room, to help your child feel secure in space.

Chapter 22

Staying in Bed

Often, when a child is young, parents don't strenuously object to him sleeping in their bed. Exhausted parents will naturally allow a child to either begin the night in their bed or stay in it if he comes to their room in the middle of the night. Suddenly, the child is 8 or 9 years old (or even older), and this pattern has become well established and is extremely difficult to break. Some children with ASD or obsessive-compulsive disorder (OCD) feel compelled to get out of bed to participate in rituals and routines, resulting in a lack of sleep or increased anxiety. The restless, active child may require less sleep than other family members, so he gets up to play or to watch television. As with most behaviors, it is important to identify where and when to "pick your battles." If this is an area of major conflict between parents, or it disrupts the siblings' sleep, and the family agrees that this behavior is a problem for everyone, then strategies and a plan of response are in order.

(**Solutions**)

- If there are two parents and caregivers in the home, it is important to have a "game plan" that both can agree to and execute.

- Small children can be carried back to their beds without discussion or social interaction. This may need to be repeated several times before it takes effect. Consider starting this approach on a Friday night. Your sleep requirement will be less, without the obligation of getting up early for work.

- Use a positive reward system to encourage your child to stay in his bed. Initially, reward him for staying in his bed for one night or even for a few hours. Then, as he improves, raise the expectation to two nights, and so on.

- The child with ASD or OCD will perseverate more when he is anxious. Try the calming strategies in Appendix A and communicate with his teacher to reduce anxiety at school.

- Some children can learn to defer sleeping in the parents' bed or room to the weekend. Establish an agreement that if your child sleeps in his own bed during the week, he will be rewarded with a weekend "sleepover" in your room.

● Consider allowing your child who always sleeps in your bed to make a bed on the floor of your bedroom, to help him ease his way back into his own room.

Part IV

Community Outings

Taking a child with special needs out into the community can be a daunting undertaking that is filled with uncertainty, stress, and anxiety. For many families, even the anticipation of an outing can garner feelings of dread. Negative experiences that have been compounded throughout multiple attempts to take children to the mall, a restaurant, the grocery store, and dentist and doctor appointments include meltdowns, tantrums, and icy stares and unsolicited comments from strangers. The seemingly simple chore of grocery shopping isn't simple for parents of children with special needs. Parents describe themselves as "being held hostage" in their own homes because they simply cannot muster the emotional energy it takes to plan the outing, anticipate their child's responses, and have a backup plan in case their child acts out. Some children are overwhelmed by the visual chaos, auditory stimuli, temperature changes, and odors of restaurants, grocery stores, malls, and retail stores. They react to this sensory overload by becoming increasingly dysregulated, and they may run around, grab items off shelves, cry, scream, become fearful and anxious, and even hit or touch other patrons' bodies or possessions. A child with ASD may insist upon buying a favorite toy or video every time he enters the store and have a tantrum when he is told, "not this time." A child with sensory modulation disorder is unpredictable and may act perfectly appropriately one day but have extreme challenges during the next visit. Parents feel as if they are riding a roller coaster without knowing when the ride will end, and they often have difficulty managing their *own* responses, as well as those of their child.

Visits to the pediatrician or dentist can be nightmares for all involved, including the professional. Some children have difficulty sitting and waiting for their appointment. They will become increasingly restless and make a mess of the waiting room. They can become increasingly anxious as they wait. The imposed touch of a hygienist, nurse, dentist, or physician to have teeth cleaned, receive injections, or have the ears checked is uncomfortable and even painful. While nearly all children can become anxious about going to the doctor or dentist, children with sensory issues or disabilities will have extreme reactions that vary in terms of duration and intensity. The behaviors are more intense, they last longer, and it is harder for these children to recover and return to a calm state.

Chapter 23

Grocery Stores

Grocery stores are not sensory-friendly places. The temperature varies widely from aisle to aisle. It is warm in the dry food section, cooler in the produce section, and very cold in the frozen food aisles. Most grocery stores use fluorescent lighting that flickers, hums, and emits a glaring light. The aisles have displays of food on both ends, which augment the visual chaos. Store employees can be cooking food samples that add to the odors already present in the deli or produce sections. Refrigerators and freezers make humming noises, and cold air escapes each time the doors are opened. Some children over-react to the sounds of the wheels of the grocery carts as patrons move them down the aisles. Cash registers beep continually, adding to the auditory stimuli that patrons create by moving and talking. A child with ASD might perseverate and refuse to move away from an enticing visual display, such as neon lighting or an "exit" sign. A sensory-seeking child or one with ADHD reacts by running, grabbing items, and even throwing food from the shelves. An over-responsive and sensitive child may react to the sensory overload by exhibiting a "fight, flight, or freeze" response. He may have a tantrum, become overly rigid and controlling, or seem to be paralyzed with fear.

- Take your child to the grocery store when he is in his most calm and happy state. Usually, shopping right after a long school day or at a peak time is not the best time to shop.

- Be realistic about your expectations for your child. Don't stay in the store too long or run too many errands at once.

- Start by making a short list to read to your child, or have him write the list for you and review the list before entering the store, so he is aware that the trip has an "end" to it.

- As the child's behavior improves, begin adding more items to the list and slowly extend the length of your shopping trips.

- Give your child a job to do. He can look for the item you need and put it in the cart, read your list, and cross off items as they are found.

- Ask him to push the cart for you. This will provide some calming muscle input, as well as help keep him near you.

- Some children can benefit from wearing a weighted vest or heavy backpack in the store, to help calm them and reduce hyperactivity.

- Give your child a baseball hat or visor to wear to help block out unappealing light.

- Have a predictable routine for the grocery store. Start and end on the same aisle each time you visit.

- Enlist your child's assistance in placing items onto the conveyor belt when you check out.

- Have him hold a bag of groceries while waiting for the checker to ring up the final purchases. This will help him understand that it is nearly time to return to the car.

- Bring headphones or an iPod into the store, so he can listen to calming music and screen out the auditory overload.

- Allow your child to bring a favorite toy or book to keep his hands engaged.

- Provide a favorite snack to use for oral calming and to provide positive reinforcement.

- Write a social story about the trip to help him understand the behavioral expectations and the plan for the day's visit.

● Try to shop at smaller grocery stores, when possible.

● Plan the grocery shopping during a time that you, the parent, are in an optimally calm state, so you will be able to model and transmit that to your child.

Chapter 24

Malls

Taking a child with special needs to a shopping mall is often on the "rarely or never" list for parents and caregivers. Similar to grocery store outings, the sensory stimuli found in the mall environment are overwhelming and create distress and negative behaviors. In addition to the lighting and visual chaos, many malls play music, both in the general area and inside individual stores, sometimes at a very high volume. The sheer size of a mall adds an additional concern for safety, because it can be easy for a child to run off and get lost. A sensory-seeking child or one with modulation issues may start the mall visit in a relatively calm state, only to become more and more active and aroused. Then, the child will begin to exhibit negative behaviors related to the disorganized state. A sensitive child may run away to hide, cover his ears, whine, and cry. Transitioning from store to store can be problematic, triggering tantrums and refusals. Some children are afraid of escalators and elevators, while others may insist on riding them over and over again. Some malls have play areas, and children can be over-stimulated and play roughly with other children, or they can refuse to leave the area to continue shopping. From an olfactory standpoint, odors from the perfume section, food court, and even clothing can be perceived as unpleasant or as an invitation to the sensory seeker. Many parents report that their children refuse to try on clothing because it still has the "new clothes" smell or feel to it.

Solutions

- Keep mall outings within a reasonable time frame. For most children, 1 hour is the limit.

- Practice "good mall behavior" by going to the mall for short periods when it is least congested and purchasing just one or two items. Then, you can increase the length of time as your child improves.

- If you have a small child, bring a stroller or rent one at the mall.

- Take a "sensory break" to calm your child. Try to find a quiet area to give your child a snack or have him sit in a massage chair, which are available at many malls.

- Provide oral regulators, such as a straw to chew on, a water bottle to drink from, or a crunchy snack.

- Have your child wear a baseball hat or visor to help reduce visual stimuli.

- Provide headphones or ear buds so he can listen to quiet classical music.

- Avoid going to the mall on weekends and holidays.

- Make a list or a visual schedule to help your child understand the abstract concept of time.

- Let him wear a backpack and carry shopping bags to provide deep-pressure input for calming and organizing sensory input.

- Use a tether attached to your child's clothing or wrist to address elopement and safety concerns.

- Resist the temptation to go to "just one more" store, even if your child seems to be doing well. That last store visit may topple him into meltdown mode because his sensory threshold has been met.

- By leaving on a positive note, you will create a visual memory of a happy mall experience, and your next visit is more likely to be a positive one.

- Reward positive behavior during the mall visit and afterward.

Chapter 25

Movie Theaters

Going to the movies with family and friends is a common social activity that can be challenging for children with behavioral concerns related to their disability or their sensory profile. Some kids may be fearful of the darkness in the theater, the loudness of the sound system, and the proximity of other people attending the movie. The video and audio presentation of the movie can be too unpredictable and inconsistent for the sensory-sensitive child or one with self-regulation issues. Other children might be distracted or irritated by the sound of people chewing popcorn or other snacks, and the odors might be perceived as noxious. Some children insist on sitting in a certain area, such as the very top row, and have a meltdown when another patron is seated in "their" seat. Others, such as children with ASD, may be upset if you arrive after the opening credits or previews or if you need to leave before the closing credits.

- Many theaters have special showings for audiences with special needs. Call the manager or find a local support group that might have information to guide you.

- If your child will only sit in a favorite area, be sure to arrive early, so he can get the seat he prefers.

- If your child is sensitive to loud noises, find out where the speakers are and sit farther away from them.

- Look for a dollar theater or go to a matinee. Other patrons may be more compassionate toward you and your child at a less expensive showing, and if you need to leave, you haven't spent a large amount of money.

- Try having your child use padded headphones to reduce the noise level.

- Get permission from the theater manager to bring your child's favorite snack food, to help keep him occupied and attentive.

- Bring an item that your child uses for soothing, such as a soft blanket or a favorite stuffed animal.

- If rocking is calming for your child, find a theater with chairs that can rock back and forth.

● Sit near an aisle, in case your child needs to take a break or use the restroom.

● Sitting through the credits may seem perseverative, but it can also help a child with transitions.

Chapter 26

Restaurants

Going out to eat should be, and can be, a positive social experience for families and friends. However, there are several issues that can arise, and parents can be left feeling disappointed, frustrated, and angry. Siblings or a parent who desired a nice birthday dinner may feel upset when a child with negative behavior disrupts and spoils the event. There are several impediments to a successful restaurant experience, including a child's restricted diet; over-reactivity to the visual, auditory, and olfactory sensory input; challenges with waiting for food to arrive; and having to remain seated for an entire meal. In addition, an unruly child naturally irritates other people who go to a restaurant to enjoy a quiet meal.

Solutions

- Many restaurants offer a gluten-free menu, or they will be happy to warm up food that you bring from home.

- Before going to a restaurant for lunch or dinner, take your child during a nonpeak time, when it is nearly empty. Let him have a small snack or a beverage to get some information about his response to the environment.

- Try to schedule restaurant meals early in the evening or during the week, when it is less busy.

- Look for seating in a low-traffic area. Avoid sitting by the servers' station or near the restroom or front door.

- If your child eats quickly and has challenges waiting for the rest of the family to finish, save a portion of his meal in an unobtrusive area and give him a few bites at a time.

- Some children are happily occupied with a class full of crushed ice to eat while waiting for the food to arrive. This is a good alternative to crackers or other food, because it won't spoil their appetite.

- Headphones, hats, and visors can be used to decrease auditory and visual stimuli in the restaurant.

- Bring a bag with activities, such as puzzles, crayons, books, or an iPad, for your child to entertain himself with at the table if he is starting to exhibit challenges with sitting or waiting.

- Help him line up, sort, or stack sugar and sugar-substitute packets to distract him and to give him a closed-ended organizational task to help calm and organize him.

● Have a family member periodically take a restless child for a short walk around the restaurant or outside to reduce wiggling.

● Help your child write or read a social story and review it prior to going into the restaurant or during the meal, if he needs a reminder.

● Use a token economy system to reward targeted and positive restaurant behavior to add incentive for your child to behave.

● Have reasonable expectations for your child and try to end the outing on a positive note.

Chapter 27

Extracurricular Activities

Finding a sport or after-school activity that is a good fit for your child can be difficult. He may not have the prerequisite motor skills, ability to follow directions that have more than one step, self-control over his emotions and body movements, or necessary attention span for group sports, such as soccer, baseball, or basketball. Some children may express an interest in joining such a group, only to become discouraged as they become aware that their skills lag behind those of their peers. Some may have good gross-motor skills and eye-hand coordination for ball sports, but they become over-stimulated easily and can be aggressive and inattentive. Because of concrete thinking and problems with social skills and understanding others' perspectives, many of our children have significant challenges with losing games gracefully and being a good sport. They can have tantrums, pout, or shut down.

- If your child chooses a ball sport or a sport such as tennis that requires good motor skills, practice with him prior to his first practice to front-load him with some skills.

- Many coaches will volunteer extra time to work with athletes that require additional assistance.

- If your child receives adapted physical education, physical therapy, or occupational therapy at school or in a clinic, ask the professional to work on the skills that his chosen sport requires.

- Alert the coach to your child's early signs of over-arousal, so he can monitor and respond before negative behaviors occur.

- When your child becomes over-stimulated, anxious, or aggressive, encourage a "chill out" break to calm him down, so he can return and behave more appropriately.

- Review the rules of the game, as well as the behavioral expectations, with the child who needs reminders and clarifications.

- Try alternatives to group sports that are more tailored to the individual, such as swimming, track and field, cross-country running, and martial arts.

- Many communities have therapeutic horse-riding programs that build core muscle strength, aid balance, and encourage socialization.

● If your child is not athletic, rather than push him into a sport, consider enrolling him in after-school programs, such as Boy Scouts, Lego clubs, robotics, and computer or science clubs.

● Look for social-skills groups that are offered by occupational therapists, speech therapists, and other professionals. These can help teach your child appropriate social behaviors for sports and other after-school activities.

Chapter 28

Dentist and Doctor Appointments

Even adults and children without disabilities and challenges can feel anxious when preparing for and going to doctor and dentist appointments. Not knowing quite what to expect can create stress for most of us. Children with special needs might obsess and hyperfocus on the appointment for days beforehand, exhibiting increasing anxiety and distress levels. Others may simply refuse to go to the appointments. Despite a parent's cajoling, explaining, or bargaining, the child will not budge. Some children seem to be prepared for the appointment, only to dissolve into a screaming fit or inconsolable crying. Older children may be perceived as spoiled brats or immature babies by professionals who are not aware of the challenges the children have, owing to their disability. Some kids are fearful of changes in their head position and will have an extreme reaction when the dentist chair begins to tip back. Others are sensitive to the strong odors in doctors' and dentists' offices. The sound of the dental hygienist's teeth-cleaning equipment may seem extremely loud or be perceived as painful to a child's auditory system. The taste or texture of the cleaning gel may cause a child to gag.

Solutions

- If your child is obsessive, try not to over-explain or talk too much about the appointment too far in advance. This can backfire and bring too much attention to the appointment.

- Social stories are helpful to prepare some children.

- Practice having the appointment at home with siblings or friends, by using a calm and playful manner to take away the mystery. First, have your child pretend to be the professional and clean the teeth, check the heartbeat and ears, and so on. Then, have him be the patient.

- Ask the doctor or dentist if your child can have the first or last appointment of the day, when there are fewer people in the waiting room.

- Talk to the dentist or doctor before the appointment, and, out of hearing range of your child, tell the specialist about the challenges your child has. This way, he or she will get a sense of his or her ability to help your child.

- Before the appointment, ask the dentist for samples of the various flavors of teeth-cleaning gel. This way, your child can identify which one is acceptable, and he will have time to get used to it first.

● During the teeth cleaning, ask the hygienist to count your child's teeth as she cleans, by using a firm, calm, and rhythmic tone. Counting is predictable and regulatory for the anxious child, and it helps him understand when the task will be completed.

● Ask the doctor or dentist to let your child sit upright or in your lap during examinations and cleanings.

● Remind the people in the room to let one person talk at a time, and that person should remain calm and confident. Too many people trying to help calm the child by talking will add to the sensory overload.

● If your child has a trusting relationship with his occupational therapist, another therapist, older sibling, or teacher, ask him or her to attend the appointment with you to help keep your child calm. Sometimes parents can naturally become too emotional and can inadvertently add to the child's anxiety.

Part V

Family and Friends

The occupational therapy profession is holistic in nature, and professionals that work with children who have special needs, whether those needs are physical, emotional, developmental, or behavioral in nature, emphasize the context in which that child functions and lives. Parents, caregivers, siblings, and friends of a child with a disability can feel stressed, overwhelmed, and anxious as they respond to and make adjustments to a child that is unpredictable and challenging. The term "family held hostage" can be used to describe how far-reaching the issues of the special-needs child can be. It can be very challenging for a child with sensory issues, ADHD, or ASD to attend birthday parties, have a playdate, and maintain a calm state during family get-togethers. So, when that child has difficulty with self-regulation and sensory modulation, understanding and following directions, or participating in community and family events, it is not just the child who is affected.

Parents may feel embarrassed or judged by strangers or other family members when their child has a meltdown in the grocery store or at Christmas dinner. They might be experiencing significant financial and emotional strain to ensure their child receives appropriate support and services at school, at home, and in the community. Siblings can feel excluded, because their brother or sister demands an excessive amount of time and attention from their parents. Some siblings develop a pattern of feeling obligated to put their own needs aside in a well-intentioned attempt to ease the parental strain they are witnessing. Other siblings may start to act out to get attention. Grandparents or other family members may not fully understand the nature of the disability and how it affects behavior. They may avoid being around the child or give unsolicited advice.

Families and friends need support and knowledge to prepare and equip them to live and interact with the special-needs child and to help that child be a happy, more effective, and more engaged member of the family.

Chapter 29

Family Gatherings

Family traditions and get-togethers are generally something to look forward to with great anticipation. However, the family who has a child that dashes from room to room, running at full speed, knocking items off tables and shelves, and pushing siblings, friends, or cousins will often dread the family event. The family members have a difficult time relaxing, hoping their child doesn't create a scene or do some damage to the home. They will be hypervigilant as they "watch and wait" for a meltdown. Families of the sensitive, sensory over-responsive and avoidant child that refuses to attend a family gathering or disappears into a back bedroom to read a book can be viewed as overly permissive, allowing their child to be "rude or antisocial." Rigid and ritualistic behaviors of a child with ASD can interfere with the planned events, and family members who don't understand the nature of autism can unwittingly or even overtly become critical or impatient.

Solutions

- "Heavy-work" exercise that involves the big muscle groups of the trunk, legs, and arms can be done prior to the event. This will decrease the sensory-seeking behaviors and decrease the anxiety of the sensory over-responsive child.

- Try to arrive before most of the other guests to avoid the auditory chaos.

- Watch your child for signs of overarousal and help him take a break if he needs one. You can take a walk outside or go to a quiet room to watch TV, listen to music, assemble Legos, or read.

- Bring favorite and familiar alternatives for your child to eat. He may be able to sit at the table if he doesn't also have to worry about eating nondesirable foods.

- Be realistic about the length of time your child can stay at the event. Try to leave when your child is doing well, so you end the event on a positive note.

- When possible, before the event, send an e-mail and remind family members and friends that your child might have some challenges and that you are grateful for their support.

Chapter 30

Holidays

Thanksgiving, Christmas, Hanukkah, New Year's, and the Fourth of July are exciting events that can be quite problematic for families. The normal routine is disrupted and changed: There is no school, bedtimes aren't strictly enforced, and mealtimes and menus may be variable. Lack of structure during the holidays can throw kids with special needs into a tailspin. The auditory and visual chaos caused by having numerous people in the house can over-stimulate your child, who can respond by being hyperactive and aggressive, fearful and avoidant, or rigid and controlling. The sight, smell, and taste of new foods can cause a child to gag, make rude comments, or run away from the table. The sound and sight of shiny wrapping paper as it is torn off packages can overwhelm a sensitive child, but a sensory-seeking child views it as an invitation to throw, rip, crush, and jump into it. As the event progresses, the avoidant or seeking behaviors increase, until the child throws a tantrum, begins to cry and whine, or hides from others. The sensation and odors of new or special clothing can create a major meltdown. Holiday food is unfamiliar, and a child may inadvertently insult a relative who prepared a special dish by refusing to eat it, spitting it out, or making a rude comment.

Solutions

- It is helpful for parents to be aware of their own arousal state. To be aware of and able to address their child's behaviors, parents need to be in a calm, non-reactive state.

- Identify which caregiver is feeling most equipped to provide supervision and support for the child, and take a break when it becomes difficult to be aware and patient.

- Don't hover around your child and impart a sense of anxiety by being overly vigilant, but keep a watchful eye for signs of overarousal from a distance.

- Prepare your child for the event by hosting a mock Thanksgiving or Christmas dinner at your house and practicing the expected behavior.

- Don't force your child to wear clothes that are uncomfortable. If he has a familiar and soothing item of clothing on, he may be able to participate in the holiday event more fully.

- If he does need to wear a new outfit for a family photo, wash the new clothes several times or have him shop with you to find an item that feels the best on his body.

● Allow your child to retreat or find a quiet place to be alone for periods to recover from the sensations of the day. Don't expect him to stay in a large, noisy group for long periods of time.

● Bring headphones or earplugs to help decrease the volume of noise.

● Let him sit at the end of the table, rather than in between people who may accidently bump him.

● Have your child assist in setting the table, clearing the dishes, or throwing wrapping paper away to give him a closed-ended job to focus on.

Chapter 31

Vacations

Going to the beach, a mountain cabin, or Disneyland or to visit family in another city or state can be a tremendous amount of fun. Staying in a hotel, eating at restaurants, visiting museums, and playing in the ocean are memories shared by many families. Unfortunately, these events are not always so happy for the family of a child with a disability. Their child might be completely overwhelmed by the stimulation of a place like Disneyland. He may dislike the feel of sand on his feet, have difficulty falling asleep in an unfamiliar bed, lack safety awareness in a large crowd, and even get separated from his family. Waiting in long lines can be nearly impossible. Options for food that the child can eat at a restaurant may be limited. Behaviors such as running away, being too loud, having a tantrum, perseverating on a favorite ride, and flopping on the ground are commonly increased during family vacations.

Solutions

- Investigate options like getting a special pass at Disneyland or finding vacation packages that specialize in providing vacations for children with disabilities.

- Go on the Internet with your child before you travel to find pictures of the vacation locale and hotel to help him create a visual of what to expect.

- Put the vacation date on the family calendar at home and periodically remind your child about the dates.

- Try to develop and implement a predictable routine and schedule for each vacation day and review it daily with your child.

- Don't try to pack too many events into one day; build in time to relax and regroup.

- Bring your child's bedding and pillow from home so he has something familiar and comfortable to rely upon in an unfamiliar setting.

- Bring a small fan to create "white noise" in the hotel room.

- If the hotel doesn't have blackout curtains, consider packing blankets or towels to block noise and light from the windows.

Chapter 32

Car and Air Travel

Parents report a variety of challenges when traveling with their child in a car, such as difficulty with sitting still and remaining seated, unbuckling the seatbelt or door locks, repeatedly rolling windows down and up, having tantrums if the parent drives a different way to school or to run errands, having conflicts with siblings, and even hitting or throwing items at the parent driver. Air travel can also be challenging. Going through security checkpoints, waiting in a crowded airport, having a lack of safety awareness, turning off electronics for takeoff and landing, and remaining buckled in the seat can be difficult for our children. Negative reactions arising from the change in routine, trying to understand unfamiliar expectations and experiences, and sensory overload can stimulate behaviors such as crying, running off, getting out of the seat, and disrupting other air travelers.

Solutions

- Help your child stay occupied with a favorite toy or electronic device, music, books, and snacks.

- Try to take hourly breaks to get out of the car to provide an appropriate movement break.

- Use the safety locks for windows and locks when possible or put strong duct tape over door locks, handles, and window switches.

- Purchase a car seat lock cover.

- Consider a car seat canopy or light blankets to provide a tentlike effect to aid in maintaining a calm state and decreasing sensory stimuli.

- Separate siblings with large pillows.

- When possible, move the back seat away from the driver to decrease the possibility of inappropriate touching.

- Review the travel plans by using visual aids or social stories.

- Simulate a car or airplane at home by using your furniture. Demonstrate events and appropriate behavior for the trip.

- Wear slip-on shoes for easy removal at airport security checkpoints.

- Find a quiet place to wait for the flight. Ask the gate attendant to page you by name when it is time to board.

- Call the airline prior to your trip to find out if they will allow the use of electronics during takeoff and landing.

- Bring a favorite pillow or blanket from home to use on the flight.

- Bring your child's car seat for air travel, so he has a familiar and comfortable place to sit and rest his head.

Chapter 33

Pets

A child with ADHD or one who is sensory seeking or sensory under-responsive, who lacks awareness and registration of the appropriate force behind his movements, might play with or squeeze a dog or cat too roughly, pull tails, try to pick up and carry an unwilling pet, and put his face too close to the animal's face. Other children, who are timid and sensitive, may be excessively fearful of pets' movements, smells, and sounds, and they may run away, cry, cover their ears, have a high anxiety level, or become irritable and angry. Some children beg and plead to get a pet, promising to take good care of it, but they lack the organizational skills to remember to feed, walk, or clean up after their pet.

Solutions

- Before obtaining a pet, borrow a similar one from a friend or family member for a few days to observe your child's responses.

- By using an amenable pet, practice the correct way to approach and handle it and get used to a pet's movements and odors.

- Terms such as "nice touch" and "gentle" are abstract, and your child may not understand them. Have your child demonstrate applying the correct touch force on your arm.

- Demonstrate rough versus gentle touch on your child's arm and head and ask him questions to raise his awareness: "Is this the right way to touch your dog?"

- Watch for signs of overarousal during play with pets and have your child take a break.

- Help your child remember the sequence of caring for his pet by using visual cues, such as a chart or checklist. Have him help you make the chart, so he can list and use words that he chooses.

- Rather than verbally telling your child each step, ask him questions to raise his awareness and to help him remember: "Is the dog's bowl full or empty?"

- If your child is sensitive to touch or odors, let him wear gloves to scoop food or animal droppings. He can also use a nose plug.

Chapter 34

Sibling Relationships

Being a sibling of a brother or sister with special needs can be gratifying, but it can often be confusing, embarrassing, and distressing. Siblings may feel neglected or ignored, as parents must focus extra time and attention on the child with a disability. Other siblings assume a parental, care-giving role, even if their parents attempt to discourage that response. Occasionally, a sibling might begin to act out or misbehave to gain attention. Some may avoid having friends come to visit or spend the night because they want to protect their sibling from stares and comments, or they may be embarrassed by the sibling's odd or unpleasant behaviors.

Solutions

- Use age-appropriate terminology to explain the diagnosis and describe the challenges to the sibling, to decrease the uncertainty and mystery.

- Try to set time aside for the nondisabled sibling. A short walk before bed may be sufficient, and you can give him your undivided attention.

- If possible, find a support group for siblings, or start your own.

- Empathize with your child if he expresses embarrassment. Remember that this is a natural response that can be worked through.

- Ask your occupational therapist or other therapist to occasionally include the nondisabled peer in a therapy session. Too often, the sibling must sit and watch his brother or sister having fun during therapy.

- Make a plan for playdates or sleepovers. Reassure your child that you will try to honor his need for socialization with his friends. It is not necessary to include the disabled sibling in all the activities.

- Help your child develop language to respond to a friend's curiosity: "My brother has autism, so it's hard for him to be around a lot of people, but he's pretty special to me."

Chapter 35

Playdates and Socializing

Parents of children with special needs express many desires and they advocate for a number of things: appropriate school placement and services, necessary therapies, increased independence with activities of daily living, and health and nutrition matters. In addition to those concerns, parents simply want their child to be happy and have friends. Some children prefer to have limited social interaction, while others crave it, but they may lack the proper skills to make and keep friends. Having a friend over to one's house for a playdate is a common activity for children in preschool and elementary school, but it is often quite difficult for kids with attention-deficit disorder, ADHD, sensory issues, or ASD. They may dominate a conversation, insist on playing favorite video games for hours, be a poor sport, have poor social skills, lack motor coordination for games, become excessively hyperactive and over-stimulated, or simply ignore the peer.

- Begin with a short playdate that includes your child's favorite activity, either at home or in the community. Limit the initial attempt to 2-3 hours, then increase the length of time as your child exhibits success and confidence.

- If your young child has difficulty initiating play with a peer, consider enlisting the support of a sibling or join the activity until it gets started. Then, fade your presence.

- For older children, try not to hover, but supervise from a distance and be aware of any overstimulation signs that your child exhibits. Step in before it escalates.

- If your child is perseverative or a very poor loser with video games, help him choose an alternative activity before the friend arrives and remove the option to play video games.

- Occasionally, a very social parent benefits from a reminder that her child's social needs are not the same as hers. For some children, being around peers all day long at school is as much as they can handle, and they need solitary time at home to recover.

- Consider fostering social engagement on a weekend, rather than a school night.

- Ask your child's occupational therapist, speech therapist, or other professional to work on play and social skills to help him navigate the complexities of peer interaction and learn skills prior to trying to generalize them to the community or home setting.

Appendix A

Calming and Alerting Activities and Ideas

These ideas have the following important components:

1. They can be done at home and at school.

2. They are inexpensive.

3. Most homes and schools have the materials on hand.

4. They can be done individually or in a group.

5. They are play based and intrinsically motivating.

Note: Before beginning any of these activities, review the following rules with your child:

1. Keep control of your body.

2. If anyone says, "Stop," you do so immediately.

3. Keep your voice quiet to help you focus on what is going on with your body.

4. Don't forget to breathe!

5. HAVE FUN!

Therapy Ball Activities:

● Wheelbarrow walk, with or without assistance.

● Jump on the ball with assistance.

● Balance on all fours, sit on tall knees, or get into a standing position with help from an adult.

● Lift the ball high above the head to throw, bounce, or roll it to a friend.

● "Push, push, push" the ball against a therapist or a peer by using arms or legs.

● Have the child "kick to the sky," where he lies on his back on the floor to kick the dropped ball straight up.

Superman: Lie on the stomach, and hold arms and legs straight out and off the floor. Try to hold this position as long as possible. Then, try to "fly."

Roly Polies: Have the child lie on his back and bend his knees toward his head. He should crunch his body up as much as he can *without* holding his legs. Have him roll back and forth and side to side, trying to keep his head and knees close together.

Chair Liftoffs: Have the child sit on a hard chair with her back straight. She should put her hands on the edges, by her hips, with her thumbs pointing forward. Then she pushes her arms HARD until her bottom lifts off the chair. Have her try to hold this position as long as possible.

Sampson: Have the child stand by a blank wall, facing forward. He should back up about 4 or 5 feet and put his hands on the wall at shoulder height. He will be leaning into the wall, holding his body up, and his elbows will be straight. Keeping his back straight, he should do pushups by bending and straightening his elbows. He can pretend he's trying to push the wall down.

Quicksand: Hold your child's feet at the ankles when he is in a four-point kneeling position. Have him crawl to the designated "land," while you provide resistance to make the muscles of his legs, trunk, and arms really work hard to move him forward.

Chin-ups: Purchase an adjustable chin-up bar at a sporting goods store to hang in a bedroom or classroom doorway, so your child can practice doing chin-ups.

Dog Pile: Take turns piling onto each other and lying on the bottom of the pile, while others lie on top. Try to get out from beneath the pile.

Playing "Get Off of Me": One person lies on top of another, who is lying on his stomach. The person on the bottom tries to push himself up into a kneeling position to tip the top person off.

Pillows and Beanbags: Put as many pillows on top of the child as he desires when he is lying on his stomach on the floor. Apply even, rhythmic pressure to his back at the pace of a slow heartbeat.

Hugs and Squeezes: Use your arms to apply deep, consistent pressure to the child's shoulders and ribcage.

Chair Rides: The child can stand behind a chair with you or a peer seated in it, to push you around the "road."

Hideout: Offer a quiet getaway space, such as a small tent, a closet, or a bed to crawl under.

Calm-Down Breathing: Have the child breathe in through the nose and out through the lips, so she can hear the "wind."

Yoga: Classes for children will help them learn about their bodies and achieve a quiet, clear consciousness.

Reducing Environmental Clutter: Tone down visual, auditory, olfactory, and tactile inputs in your environment by removing unnecessary clutter.

Repetitive, Closed-Ended Tasks: Offer your child sorting, organizing, categorizing, and counting tasks that have a clear beginning and end. This will help your child achieve a calm state.

Backward Chaining Example for Dressing

Parents and caregivers generally allow their child to begin a dressing task. Then, they will step in and finish the task when the child experiences frustration and difficulty. The concept of "backward chaining" offers assistance at the beginning of the task, rather than at the completion of it. With this approach, the child will remember that he, not the parent, completed the dressing task, and he will experience mastery and a willingness to attempt the task the next day. In addition to having a positive experience with task completion, this approach will reduce frustration behaviors and help a child persist and feel successful.

Example: Backward Chaining for Putting On Pants

Initial Sequence—Helping with All Steps

1. With your child seated, help him put his legs through the openings in the pants. Pull the fabric over his feet until they show.

2. Use the phrase, "One foot out, two feet out, stand up, pull up" to help him learn the sequence.

3. When he is standing, position his hands in the front of the pants and place your hands at the back of the pants. Help him pull the pants from his feet up to his waist.

Second Sequence—Reducing Your Support at the End

1. With your child seated, help him put his legs through the openings in the pants. Pull the fabric over his feet until they show.

2. Use the phrase, "One foot out, two feet out, stand up, pull up" to help him learn the sequence.

3. When he is standing, position his hands in the front of the pants, and place your hands at the back of the pants. Help him pull the pants up to his hips.

4. Let him finish by independently pulling the pants up from his hips to his waist.

Third Sequence—Continuing to Reduce Support

1. With your child seated, help him put his legs through the openings in the pants. Pull the fabric over his feet until they show.

2. Use the phrase, "One foot out, two feet out, stand up, pull up" to help him learn the sequence.

3. When he is standing, position his hands in the front of the pants, and place your hands at the back of the pants. Help him pull his pants up to his thighs, above his knees.

4. Let him finish by independently pulling his pants up from his thighs to his waist.

Fourth Sequence—Reduce Your Support Further

1. With your child seated, help him put his legs through the openings in the pants. Pull the fabric over his feet until they show.

2. Use the phrase, "One foot out, two feet out, stand up, pull up" to help him learn the sequence.

3. When your child is standing, position his hands in the front of the pants, and place your hands at the back of the pants. Help him pull the pants up to just below his knees.

4. Let him finish by independently pulling the pants up from below his knees to his waist.

Fifth Sequence

1. With your child seated, help him put his legs through the openings in the pants. Pull the fabric over his feet until they show.

2. Use the phrase, "One foot out, two feet out, stand up, pull up" to help him learn the sequence.

3. When your child is standing, position his hands in the front of the pants, and place your hands at the back of the pants. Help him pull the pants up to just over his feet.

4. Let him finish by independently pulling the pants up from his feet to his waist.

Final Sequence

Provide verbal cueing only to help him with the steps.

Example of a Visual Schedule for the Morning Routine

Here is a sample visual schedule your child can refer to in the morning, as he gets himself ready for the day.

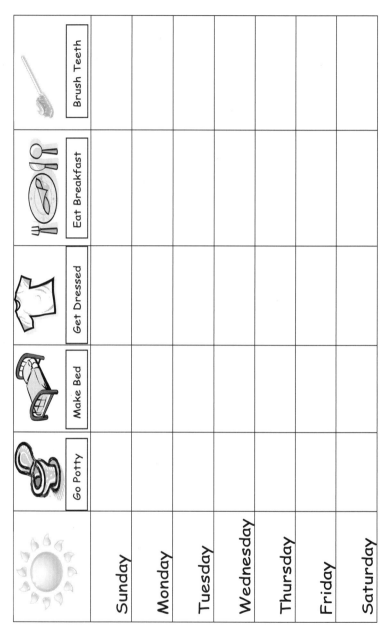

	Go Potty	Make Bed	Get Dressed	Eat Breakfast	Brush Teeth
Sunday					
Monday					
Tuesday					
Wednesday					
Thursday					
Friday					
Saturday					

Note: It is often helpful to use photographs of your child's actual items, or of him completing the task.

Example of a Visual Schedule for the Night Routine

Your child can use a visual schedule to complete his evening routine, like the one provided here.

My Bedtime Chart

	Clean Up Toys
	Take a Bath
	Put on Pajamas
	Brush Teeth
	Drink of Water
	Potty Time
	Read a Book
	Sleep Time

Note: It is often helpful to use photographs of your child's actual items, or of him completing the task.

Appendix E

Fun and Easy Activities to Develop Fine-Motor Skills

These activities develop hand arches, separation of the fingers, and finger isolation. They improve manipulative abilities for self-care and handwriting, and they strengthen the hand muscles.

Use tweezers to eat snack foods, such as popcorn or mini-marshmallows.

Use medicine droppers to transfer liquid from one area to another. (Styrofoam egg cartons work well for this.)

Make a "bank" out of a plastic butter tub. Cut a thin slot in the top cover and have the child put coins through the slot. It should be thin enough to offer some resistance.

Play "hide and seek" with coins. Put two to six nickels on the table. Have your child pick them up one at a time, storing them in his hand until all are stored. Then, have him place them back on the table one at a time, trying not to drop them.

Play the "flicking game." Put small items on a tabletop, and then have your child curl his fingers in and "flick" the items with his index finger and thumb.

Have the child flip playing cards over to match and/or sort them.

Put stickers on your child's body, and have him remove them with his "pinchy fingers" (thumb and index finger). Increase the challenge by having him remove the stickers with his eyes closed.

Hide objects in his clothing and have him locate them by "feel," without looking.

Have your child place and remove clothespins on the edges of a large, thick piece of cardboard or a round plastic lid, such as one from a margarine container (this strengthens pinching). To make it more fun and interesting, have the child put the clothespins on his clothing or on yours.

Play tug-of-war and the "fishing game." In the "fishing game," the child holds onto a rope, while an adult pulls him "to shore." (These games strengthen the ability to grasp.)

Have your child shake dice in his cupped hands. Have him close his eyes to see if he can hear the dice clanking together.

Commercial games, such as "Don't Break the Ice," "Perfection," "Oreo Cookies," mosaic tiles, Legos, K'nex, Pick-Up Sticks, and jacks are fun and therapeutic.

Have your child carry heavy groceries.

Have your child use a squeeze bottle to help clean mirrors or play in the bathtub.

Continue to encourage and expect the highest level possible from your child with regard to self-care activities, such as manipulating open containers, lids, and baggies, dressing, and so on.

Glossary

ADHD: Attention-deficit/hyperactivity disorder

ASD: Autism spectrum disorder

Sensory modulation disorder:

- Dysregulated responses to sensory input from the environment and to the body

- Unpredictable responses

- Responses that are too slow, too fast, and variable within and between sensory systems

Sensory over-responsiveness:

- Exaggerated responses to sensation

- Oversensitivity to stimulation from various systems

- Atypical, sometimes dramatic, responses to noise, touch, movement, light, and smells

Sensory Processing Disorder:

- Maladaptive responses to sensory input from the environment and the body

- Challenges with responding to sensory stimuli appropriately, which affects motor function; the emotional, affective state; and arousal and attention

Sensory seeking or sensory craving:

- Excessively seeking out sensory stimuli through movement, touch, sound, and smells

- Seeking and craving behavior results in an increased state of disorganization

Sensory under-responsiveness:

- Reduced awareness of sensory stimuli to various systems

- Slow response to sensory input

- Lessened sensitivity to touch, sound, movement, and visual information, as compared with peers

Additional Resources

The *Out-of-Sync* books by Carol Kranowitz

Just Take a Bite by Lori Ernsperger and Tania Stegen-Hanson

Sensory Parenting by Britt Collins and Jackie Linder Olson

Toilet Training for Individuals with Autism by Maria Wheeler

No Longer A SECRET by Doreit Bialer and Lucy Jane Miller

"Move About Activity Cards" by David and Kathy Jereb

The New Social Story Book by Carol Gray

Sensational Kids by Lucy Jane Miller

"Yoga for Children with Special Needs" by Aras Baskauskas, with Britt Collins

How to Teach Life Skills to Kids with Autism or Asperger's by Jennifer McIlwee Myers

About the Author

Beth Aune, OTR/L, is an occupational therapist and owner of Desert Occupational Therapy for Kids, a pediatric outpatient clinic. Beth and her team of dedicated and passionate professionals provide assessment and intervention for at-risk children with a variety of diagnoses, including autism spectrum disorder, Sensory Processing Disorder, developmental delay, feeding dysfunction, Down syndrome, cerebral palsy, and others. Beth and Desert OT for Kids provide therapy to children in the home and in clinical and educational settings.

Beth is a coauthor of *Behavior Solutions for the Inclusive Classroom* (2010) and *More Behavior Solutions In and Be-*

yond the Inclusive Classroom (2011). She speaks all over the United States on the topic of practical solutions and strategies for teachers and parents to develop an understanding of sensory processing and to address challenging behaviors in the school setting and at home.

Beth and her team of occupational therapists are dedicated to helping children achieve their highest potential in their daily functioning, with an emphasis on partnership with parents, caregivers, and teachers. She is passionate about her profession as an occupational therapist and considers it a calling.